Political Parties in the United States

Harcourt
SCHOOL PUBLISHERS

Visit *The Learning Site!* www.harcourtschool.com

The Two-Party System

If you wanted to become President of the United States, what is one of the first things you would need to do? Join a political party.

A political party is a group of people who share ideas about how the government should work. They organize to elect candidates who share their goals. Most government leaders today are in either the Democratic party or the Republican party.

For most of its history, the United States has had two main parties. The names and ideas of the parties have changed, but not often have there been more than two major parties to choose from. When a new party has appeared, it has often disappeared quickly. Sometimes, though, a new party has replaced an old one that was fading away.

People show support for their political party.

Party Symbols

The symbol of the Republican party is an elephant. The symbol of the Democratic party is a donkey. At first, these symbols were used to make fun of the parties. When the Democrat Andrew Jackson ran for President in 1827, people compared him to a donkey because of his stubbornness. Then, a cartoonist made fun of Republicans by showing them as a frightened elephant running away from a donkey wearing a lion's suit. In time, both parties changed the jokes into symbols for their parties.

An early political cartoon of the Republican party

One reason that political parties are so important is the United States' "winner-take-all" way of choosing leaders. The party that wins the most votes for an office gets its candidate elected. If your party gets just one more vote than the other party, your candidate wins. There is no prize for second place.

The Party Platform

Political parties explain their ideas and goals in a document called a "platform." Usually, a platform is something a person stands on. A political platform is what a party stands for.

Writing a party's platform requires compromises. Members of a party seldom agree about everything. A platform lists the ideas that *most* of the party agrees with, at least for a while.

Senator Barack Obama presented the Democrats' platform at the Democratic National Convention in 2004.

3

Merchants Against Farmers

Even though political parties are important today, the Constitution says nothing about them. In fact, the founders who wrote the Constitution hoped political parties would never arise in the United States. They feared that this kind of division would hurt the country. The founders hoped that everyone would work together for the good of all. But differences of opinion in the country's free society led to political parties anyway.

The founders themselves disagreed about what "the good of all" really was. They had different ideas about what kind of country the United States should be and how it should be run.

People who supported the new Constitution were called Federalists. They wanted a strong federal government to unite the nation. They pictured a large country with bustling towns full of trade. Wealthy merchants, business owners, and shopkeepers supported the Federalists. So did some rich plantation owners in the southern states.

| The First Political Parties ||
Federalists	Democratic-Republicans
Leaders: John Adams, Alexander Hamilton	Leaders: Thomas Jefferson, James Madison, James Monroe
Focus: the elite	Focus: the common man
Federal strength	States' rights
Urban vision	Agrarian vision
Favored indirect elections and long terms in office	Favored direct elections and short terms in office
Model: Britain	Model: France

Other people disagreed. The Democratic-Republicans wanted to keep things small and simple. They were mostly farmers or people from small villages. The Democratic-Republicans pictured a country where most people lived in small towns and government stayed close to the people it served. The Democratic-Republicans did not trust a powerful federal government. To them, a strong President seemed too much like a king.

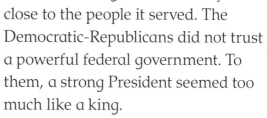
John Adams

George Washington did not say which side he supported, but both the Federalists and Democratic-Republicans trusted him. He was so respected that he was elected unanimously to two terms as President. The second President, Federalist John Adams, was not as popular. In 1800, at the end of his first term, even the Federalists were divided over whether to re-elect him.

Meanwhile, Thomas Jefferson generally found himself on the side of the Democratic-Republicans. He shared their liking for small towns and farm life. He feared that a strong government would be a threat to liberty. The Democratic-Republicans supported Jefferson. They soon became known as Jeffersonian Republicans.

Thomas Jefferson

The Jeffersonian Triumph

The election of 1800 was very close. Jeffersonians thought Adams and the Federalists were becoming tyrants. Federalists said that if Jefferson became President, it would lead to mob rule. Thomas Jefferson was elected by a slim margin, partly because the Federalists had not been able to agree on one candidate.

People feared that the transfer of power might not be peaceful. Jefferson tried to unite the country. "Every difference of opinion is not a difference of principle," he said. "We are all Republicans—we are all Federalists." The transfer of power went peacefully. But the differences of opinion did not go away.

Thomas Jefferson arriving at his inauguration

In those days, only a few people's opinions cou[nt]. [In] most of the country, only white men who owned lan[d] could vote. This was the group that formed political p[arties.]

Meanwhile, the split between the Federalists and t[he] Jeffersonian Republicans deepened. When the War of 1812 with Britain began, Federalist merchants and business leaders opposed it because it was bad for trade. Most Jeffersonian Republicans supported the war.

In 1814, Federalists in New England got together at a meeting called the Hartford Convention. They threatened to break away from the United States because of the war. The threat came to nothing, and the war ended a few weeks later. However, the Hartford Convention made the Federalists look disloyal to the United States. As a consequence, the Federalist party soon faded away.

Voters on election day in Philadelphia in 1815

7

Democrats Against Whigs

With no more Federalist party, voters in 1824 found themselves with five presidential candidates to choose from—all Jeffersonian Republicans! John Quincy Adams, from New England, squeaked past Andrew Jackson, a popular war hero from the South. Jackson's supporters claimed Adams stole the election.

Four years later, Jackson and his supporters won the presidency. By then, they had also changed their party's name. Jackson's supporters now called themselves Democrats.

Andrew Jackson's election was welcomed by many people from the southern and western parts of the country. He had few supporters in the northeastern states, however. Still, Jackson considered himself the common man's President.

During Andrew Jackson's inaugural ball, a cheering mob rushed into the White House.

Because Jackson believed he spoke for the people, he often vetoed laws that Congress had passed. In fact, he vetoed more bills than all six earlier Presidents put together. Some people were alarmed by his bold use of power. They called him "King Andrew" or "King Mob."

Jackson's opponents began to call themselves "Whigs," after the anti-royal party in England. By choosing this name, they wanted to suggest that President Jackson was acting too much like a king. The Whigs said Congress, not the President, should be the stronger.

While Jackson was President, many new groups of men began to take part in politics. During the 1820s and 1830s, states began to allow nearly all white men to vote, even if they did not own a farm or a shop. As a result, more and more men became interested in political parties. Most white men over 21 years of age went eagerly to vote on election day. This change is often called "Jacksonian democracy." Still, very few African American men could vote. And no women could do so.

Some people accused Andrew Jackson of acting like a king.

Newcomers Against the Old Guard

The United States was changing. Farmers left their villages for the cities. They wanted jobs in the factories there. Immigrants from Ireland and Germany also moved into the cities. Political parties used barbecues, rallies, and songs to appeal to these voters. They organized huge parades.

At this time, the Whig party included many American-born New England Protestants. These Whigs worried about immigrants, who competed with them for jobs. They worried about issues such as slavery. They even had to worry about their own candidates. The first Whig candidate to be elected President, William Henry Harrison, died of a cold only a month into his term. And his Vice President, John Tyler, acted so un-Whiggish that the Whigs finally threw him out of the party.

The Whigs reminded voters that William Henry Harrison had been born in a log cabin.

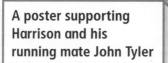

A poster supporting Harrison and his running mate John Tyler

Newspapers and Politics

Newspapers are an important part of American politics. The press is sometimes called "the fourth branch" of government—the one that keeps an eye on the other three. Today, most newspapers try to be neutral about politics in their reports. But in the 1800s, many newspapers clearly favored one party over the other. Papers often had names such as the *Greenville Democrat* or the *Springfield Republican*.

The Democrats tended to be from the South, like their hero Andrew Jackson. Many Democrats supported slavery, or at least accepted it. They also believed strongly in the westward expansion of the United States and in pushing out the Native Americans who already lived in the West. The Democratic party made a point of reaching out to immigrants, many of whom were Catholic. Democrats relied on immigrants' votes to stay in power.

Around 1850, immigration worried some Whigs so much that they decided to start a new party. They hoped to bar immigrants from voting or holding office. The new party's official name was the American party. But party members wanted to keep their identities secret, so whenever someone asked them about it, they replied, "I know nothing." It did not take long for them to be called Know-Nothings.

The Know-Nothings were a "third party," a name given to any party that is not one of the two major political parties of its time. They were successful at first, but their platform was too narrow. After 1856, the party died out.

Slave States Against Free States

Slavery soon became a huge political issue. Some Whigs wanted to end slavery at once. Southern Democrats wanted slavery to spread into new states. Northern Democrats and many Whigs wanted to keep slavery from spreading, but they did not mind if it continued in the old states. Party leaders tried to find a compromise, but none seemed to work.

Sojourner Truth gave speeches against slavery.

One group of Northern Democrats, called the Barnburners, opposed allowing slavery in new states. Abolitionists started another group, called the Liberty party. Soon these two parties joined to form the Free Soil party.

The Barnburners

The Barnburners got their name because their opponents said they were like the foolish farmer who burned down his own barn to get rid of the rats in it. Opponents said the Barnburners were destroying the Democratic party to get rid of slavery.

The turmoil threatened the Democratic party and the Whigs. The Whigs had already lost members to the Know-Nothings and the Free-Soilers. Now, another party rose to challenge the Whigs. The new party took an old name and called itself the Republican party.

12

The Republicans were against slavery. They supported a strong federal government that would help industries grow. They joined with the abolitionist Whigs, Northern Democrats, and Free-Soilers.

In the election of 1860, the Democrats could not agree on a candidate. They finally nominated one candidate for the North and a different candidate for the South. Meanwhile, the Republicans united around Abraham Lincoln.

A new party entered the contest as well. The Constitutional Union party was formed by old Southern Whigs and Know-Nothings. Its goal was simply to be neutral on slavery.

Lincoln won all the states in the North. The two Democrats and one Constitutional Unionist divided the rest of the vote among them. Under the winner-take-all system, Lincoln became President. As a consequence of Lincoln's election, the South seceded from the Union before Lincoln could even be inaugurated.

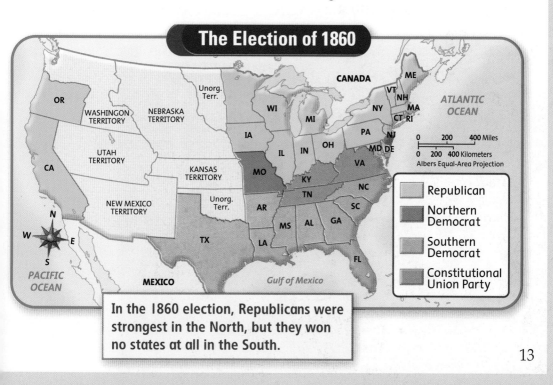

The Election of 1860

Legend:
- Republican
- Northern Democrat
- Southern Democrat
- Constitutional Union Party

In the 1860 election, Republicans were strongest in the North, but they won no states at all in the South.

13

Political Parties Today

Today's Democratic and Republican parties are very different from the two parties that existed in 1860. The way political parties select their candidates has changed, too.

Today, the election process starts with primary elections. These are state-by-state elections in which voters choose a candidate from their political party to run in the final election, which is called the general election.

In some states, voters choose candidates in a caucus. A caucus starts with a series of meetings between candidates and voters. Local party leaders then vote on behalf of the voters to select a winner.

In most primary elections, citizens vote directly for candidates. But in presidential primaries, citizens often vote for delegates. The delegates promise to vote for a certain presidential candidate at the party's national convention.

Picking a candidate during the Iowa caucus

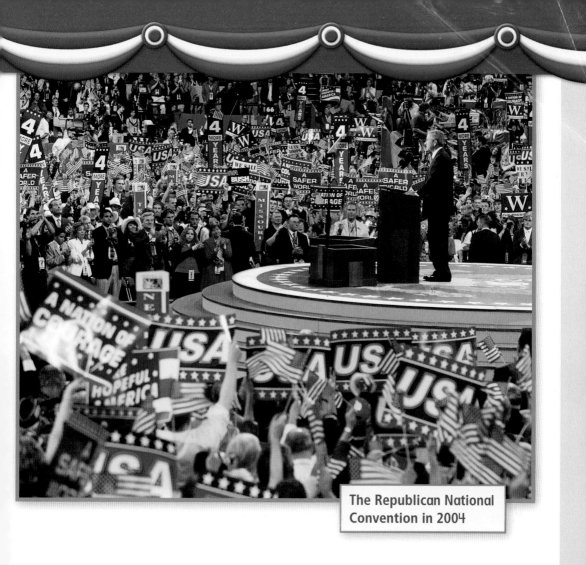

The Republican National Convention in 2004

Before the presidential election, each of the major political parties holds a national convention. At the national convention, the delegates nominate their party's candidate for President. They also decide on the party's platform.

The parades and rallies of the 1800s have given way to the political conventions we have today, where candidates are nominated and platforms are written. In this way, democracy continues in the United States.

Think and Respond

1. What is a political party?

2. What were the differences between the Federalists and the Democratic-Republicans?

3. Why did Andrew Jackson's opponents accuse him of acting like a king?

4. How did the issue of slavery change political parties in the 1850s?

5. Do you think there should be more than two major political parties? Explain why or why not.

 # Activity

Work with a group of three or four classmates to make up a new political party. Choose a name for your party. Write a platform for your party, telling what it stands for. Make a sign or a bumper sticker to encourage people to support your party.